J
232.9
K

3725

Kasuya, Masahiro

The way Christmas came

COMMUNITY PRESBYTERIAN CHURCH
PROSPECT AND NORFOLK AVENUES
CLARENDON HILLS, ILLINOIS

J
232.9
K

3725

THE WAY CHRISTMAS CAME

By Masahiro Kasuya

English text by Chieko Funakoshi

Edited by Mildred Schell

Judson Press®

© Shiko-Sha 1972
Original edition published in Japan by
Shiko-Sha Co. Ltd., Tokyo, Japan, 1972

First published in U.S.A. in 1973 by Judson Press, Valley Forge, Pa. 19481
Fourth Printing, 1977

COMMUNITY PRESBYTERIAN CHURCH
PROSPECT AND NORFOLK AVENUES
CLARENDON HILLS, ILLINOIS

Library of Congress Cataloging in Publication Data

Kasuya, Masahiro.
    The way Christmas came.

    SUMMARY: An account of the birth of Jesus.
    Translation of Kurisumasu.
    1. Jesus Christ—Nativity—Juvenile literature.
[1. Jesus Christ—Nativity] I. Funakoshi, Chieko.
II. Title.
BT315.2.K313   232.9'21 [E]   72-13014
ISBN 0-8170-0593-5

Printed in Japan by Shiko-Sha Co. Ltd., Tokyo
The name JUDSON PRESS is registered as a trademark in the U.S. Patent Office.

Mary and Joseph were going to Bethlehem.
Mary rode on the back of their friend,
  the donkey.
Joseph walked beside them.
It was a long, long trip.
Joseph and friend donkey
  walked,
    and walked,
      and walked.
Mary and Joseph and friend donkey all grew very tired.

The little town of Bethlehem is an old, old town.
Tonight something special is going to happen
   in the little town of Bethlehem.
Tonight the Christ child will be born
   in Bethlehem.
He will be called Jesus.

But no one knows Joseph and Mary.
No one knows about the special thing which will
  happen.
No one knows who will be born in Bethlehem tonight.
Bethlehem is filled with people.
There is no room for Joseph and Mary—
no room for Jesus to be born.

Mary is so tired, and Joseph is sad.
Even though the inns are full,
Joseph *must* find a place for them
 to spend the night.

At last, Joseph finds a stable where
   cows and donkeys sleep.
The hay smells sweet and clean.
There is room for Mary and Joseph and friend donkey.
They are happy to be in the stable.

In a field outside the town
   shepherds are watching over their sheep.
All is quiet in the shepherds' field.

The sheep are fast asleep.
The shepherds are growing sleepy, too.
Back in Bethlehem, all the people are
   sleeping.

But—at this very moment—
The Christ child is being born!

All at once,
the sky shines brightly with heavenly lights.
There is the sound of singing.
It is the song of the angels, singing praises
to the Christ child,
to Jesus, who is born in the manger of Bethlehem.

It is the happiest song the world has ever heard.
It is the Good News that God has sent his Son
to show the world what God's love is like.

The shepherds listen to the Good News the angels sing.
They hurry to the stable.
They want to see this Christ child who has been born.
They want to kneel before his manger
　and
　　adore
　　　him!

As the shepherds hurry to Bethlehem,
the sheep run after them.

When they reach the manger in Bethlehem,
the shepherds sing a song of glory
to praise the newborn Christ child.
They sing so loudly that the
   cows
      and
        the
          donkeys
            are surprised
and add sounds of delight to the singing.

Mary smiles with happiness.
Joseph is happy too.

After the shepherds and the sheep have gone
  back to their field,
the stable is quiet.
But it is filled with
                    HAPPINESS!

Angels and shepherds sang
prayers of thanksgiving to God
for his wonderful gift.
The prayers, long remembered by Mary
and Joseph, seemed to fill the stable with
                                        JOY!

This is the way Christmas came—
on the night when the Christ child was born.